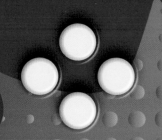

Streaming
Beginner's Guide

21st Century Skills **INNOVATION LIBRARY**

Josh Gregory

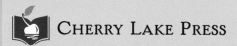
CHERRY LAKE PRESS

Published in the United States of America by Cherry Lake Publishing Group
Ann Arbor, Michigan
www.cherrylakepublishing.com

Reading Adviser: Beth Walker Gambro, MS, Ed., Reading Consultant, Yorkville, IL

Photo Credits: ©DC Studio / Shutterstock, cover, 19, 21, 29; ©Twinsterphoto / Shutterstock, 9; ©Prostock-studio / Shutterstock, 11; ©Postmodern Studio / Shutterstock, 12; ©Tada Images / Shutterstock, 14; ©Casimiro PT / Shutterstock, 15; ©Konstantin Savusia / Shutterstock, 17; ©Dragon Images / Shutterstock, 18; ©Jasni / Shutterstock, 23; ©Girts Ragelis / Shutterstock, 25; ©Devon Deth / Shutterstock, 26; ©Gorodenkoff / Shutterstock, 27; ©Krakenimages.com / Shutterstock, 30

Cherry Lake Press is an imprint of Cherry Lake Publishing Group.

Names: Gregory, Josh, author.
Title: Streaming : beginner's guide / by Josh Gregory.
Description: Ann Arbor, Michigan : Cherry Lake Press, 2023. | Series: Unofficial guides | Includes bibliographical references and index. | Audience: Grades 4-6 | Summary: "Streaming services like Twitch draw countless millions of viewers every day. Readers will learn all about the history of video game livestreaming, from its days as a niche hobby to its mainstream breakthrough. They will also find out what it takes to succeed in today's highly competitive streaming environment. Includes table of contents, author biography, sidebars, glossary, index, and informative backmatter"— Provided by publisher.
Identifiers: LCCN 2023002142 (print) | LCCN 2023002143 (ebook) | ISBN 9781668927922 (library binding) | ISBN 9781668928974 (paperback) | ISBN 9781668930441 (epub) | ISBN 9781668933404 (kindle edition) | ISBN 9781668931929 (pdf)
Subjects: LCSH: eSports (Contests)—Juvenile literature. | Streaming video—Juvenile literature. | Live streaming— Juvenile literature.
Classification: LCC GV1469.34.E86 G746 2023 (print) | LCC GV1469.34.E86 (ebook) | DDC 794.8—dc23/eng/20230227
LC record available at https://lccn.loc.gov/2023002142
LC ebook record available at https://lccn.loc.gov/2023002143

Cherry Lake Publishing Group would like to acknowledge the work of the Partnership for 21st Century Learning, a Network of Battelle for Kids. Please visit http://www.battelleforkids.org/networks/p21 for more information.

Printed in the United States of America

Note from publisher: Websites change regularly, and their future contents are outside of our control. Supervise children when conducting any recommended online searches for extended learning opportunities.

Josh Gregory is the author of more than 200 books for kids. He has written about everything from animals to technology to history. A graduate of the University of Missouri–Columbia, he currently lives in Chicago, Illinois.

Contents

CHAPTER 1

Watching People Play

Years ago, the only time people would watch others play video games was when they were in the same room as the person who was playing. They might be waiting for their own turn to play or just hanging out with some friends. But watching the game was probably not the main reason they were in the room.

Today, things are very different. Watching people play video games online via **livestream** is one of the most rapidly growing forms of entertainment in the world. Many people who don't even spend much time playing video games themselves are happy to watch for hours as their favorite creators play games and chat with viewers. At any given moment, more than two million viewers are logged into Twitch, the most popular service for streaming video games. These viewers can choose from millions of different streaming channels.

With nearly limitless variety, and more people joining the world of streaming every day, there's truly something for everyone to enjoy.

Some of the most well-known streamers became popular for their incredible skills in competitive online games. These **esports** pros impress by winning match after match in games like *Fortnite, Call of Duty,* and *Overwatch*. They make it look easy as they pull off techniques that the average player would find impossible.

The fast-paced, team-based action of *Overwatch* makes it perfect for streaming.

Being Careful Online

Twitch and other livestreaming services are highly social. Viewers watch real people, many of whom are broadcasting from their own homes. These viewers typically interact with both the streamers and with each other in a chat window next to the stream's video.

Always get a parent's or guardian's permission before watching streams. Streaming services have built-in features to help prevent kids from seeing inappropriate material. Many popular channels also have moderators to help keep the chat from getting out of hand. However, these things aren't perfect. Never share personal information online, and be sure to tell a parent or trusted adult if you ever see something that makes you uncomfortable.

Sometimes they offer tips and tricks to help other players get better at the games. Other times, they talk trash or find funny ways to brag about victories and complain about losses.

Other streamers take a very different approach. They might stick mainly to single-player games, going through each one slowly and carefully. Along the way, they might share interesting facts about how the game was made or insight into the world of game development.

Some streamers tackle single-player games in a very different way: by trying to complete them as fast as possible. These streamers, called speed runners, learn every last detail of a game and find ways to shave every possible second off their completion times. They play the same game over and over and over. They might discover glitches that allow them to skip levels or new techniques for defeating a certain enemy more quickly.

Speed runners often play classic games such as *Doom*, which was released in 1993.

Some streamers focus on a single game or type of game. Others are willing to play a wider variety. They might take on the latest releases or try to play as many classics as possible. There are even streamers who don't play games at all—they just hang out and chat with their viewers. Some streamers have gimmicks, like wearing costumes or talking in funny voices.

Multiplayer online battle arena (MOBA) games such as *League of Legends* draw huge audiences on streaming sites.

Some streamers attract fans with their unique style or sense of humor.

The most popular streamers are bona fide celebrities. They have millions of fans who follow their every move online. But for the most part, streamers are just everyday people who like to have fun by entertaining others.

CHAPTER 2

The History of Streaming

So, what changed to make people more interested in watching others play video games? One of the main reasons people didn't watch video game streams in the past was that they simply didn't exist yet.

The earliest known video livestream took place in 1993, when a group of computer **engineers** streamed footage of their band playing a live concert using experimental tech they had created. Throughout the 1990s, live-streaming technology got better and easier to use, but it still wasn't as common as it is today. Using it smoothly required a very fast internet connection—something most people did not have at the time.

In 2007, a website called Justin.tv was launched. It encouraged users to broadcast live video streams of their daily lives. One of the site's founders streamed his entire life, twenty-four hours a day, every day. But the most popular channels on Justin.tv turned out to be something completely different: video game streams.

Today, video livestreaming is so common that it can be used for kids to attend school remotely.

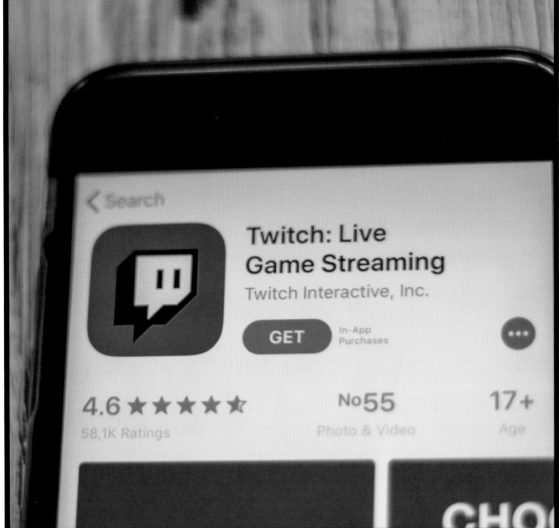

Millions and millions of people have downloaded the Twitch app.

As this section of the site grew and grew, the owners of Justin.tv decided to turn it into its own service called Twitch.tv.

Twitch quickly became the most popular place on the internet to watch gaming streams. In 2014, the service was purchased by Amazon, one of the world's largest technology companies, for almost a billion dollars. Under Amazon's ownership, Twitch started to grow faster and faster. Today, it remains the most popular video game streaming service by far.

Stuck Inside

While streaming was already on the rise, the beginning of the COVID-19 pandemic in 2020 helped kick its popularity into overdrive. Around the world, countless people were stuck at home and looking for things to do. Many of them turned to livestreaming services to pass the time. It turned out that streaming was very good at helping people feel less lonely. Not only could they enjoy exciting gaming livestreams, but they could also socialize with fellow viewers in the chat. That year, the amount of time viewers spent watching Twitch and Facebook Gaming almost doubled!

Twitch isn't the only major player in the world of streaming, though. In recent years, tech giants YouTube and Facebook have both made a big splash with their own services: YouTube Gaming

Many people believed that Mixer would provide strong competition with Twitch, but the service did not last long.

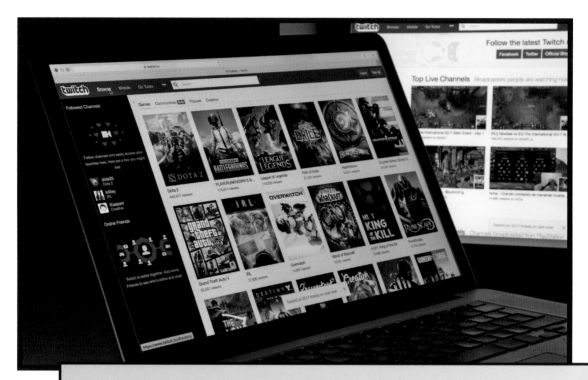

Twitch's website sorts streams by which games they feature, making it easy to browse for a specific game.

and Facebook Gaming. Before that, Microsoft tried to compete with Twitch by launching a service called Mixer. The company even went so far as to pay huge amounts of money to some of Twitch's most popular streamers to switch to the new service. However, Mixer turned out to be short-lived, and it was shut down in 2020.

CHAPTER 3

Channel Surfing

With so many options, it can be hard to decide how to spend your time watching streams. Which service should you use? Which channels should you watch? Where and when should you tune in? No matter what time of day, there is always a nearly limitless selection of live channels to watch. You can bounce from channel to channel, watching just a few minutes of each. Or you can settle in with your favorite streamer to watch for an entire evening. It all depends on what you're into.

One nice thing about livestreams is that it's easy to watch them just about anywhere, anytime, on almost any device you can think of. All you need are an internet connection and a computer, smartphone, tablet, game console, or TV with the streaming app of your choice. Then you can simply load up the app, choose a channel, and start watching for free.

Most of the important parts of Twitch and other streaming services are completely free. On Twitch, you can watch as much as you want without even creating a username or signing up for an account. But if you want to use some of the other features of your favorite streaming service, it might cost you a few dollars.

A tablet is one of the easiest and most comfortable ways to watch your favorite streams.

Most big Twitch channels allow you to pay a small monthly fee—usually around five dollars—to subscribe. This can get you a variety of things, depending on what the channel's creator offers. Usually it allows viewers to avoid watching ads. It might also grant them the use of special badges and icons in the chat, so other users will see that they are subscribers. Some channels even

Fans typically only subscribe to a small number of streamers at a time.

Money from subscriptions helps streamers pay for all the expensive equipment they use to run their channels.

have separate, subscriber-only chat rooms. Subscription fees are also a way to support streamers—part of the fee goes directly to paying them.

Another way to avoid ads is to pay a monthly fee of $8.99 to unlock Twitch Turbo. This feature allows users to skip almost all ads on every channel. However, the money from this service does not go to the streamers themselves.

Viewers who are really dedicated to a certain streamer might want to support them as much as possible. Outside of subscriptions, Twitch also offers viewers the option of buying something called Bits. Bits can be used to "cheer" during a stream when something fun happens. When you use Bits to cheer, the streamer will get money from Twitch.

Viewers might cheer for a streamer who does something exciting, such as scoring a goal in *Rocket League.*

Many streamers are all alone as they run their channels, and interaction with viewers can help them feel connected.

If you have any favorite streamers, it's easy to decide where and when to watch: simply figure out what service they use and when they stream. Most major streamers have regular schedules they post to social media so their followers know when to log on. And most of them also make sure to be online as much as they can, streaming for hours and hours almost every day.

Money Matters

While things like Bits and subscriptions are not very expensive on their own, using them frequently can really add up. Always set a budget and stick to it when paying for things on Twitch or other streaming services. This means deciding ahead of time on how much money it is OK to spend. Once you decide, there's no going back. It's a limit you need to stick to.

Always ask a parent or guardian before spending money on Twitch, an online game, or any other online service. They can help you set a budget, or they might tell you not to spend any money at all. No matter what, remember that you can have just as much fun online without spending money!

The amount of content to watch on Twitch is literally never-ending.

This means it's almost impossible to keep up with every single moment of a streamer's channel. But the upside is that you'll almost always have something new to watch when you log on.

CHAPTER 4

What It Takes

Almost anyone can get started as a streamer. All it takes is some basic equipment and a willingness to go online and perform for an audience. But creating a truly successful channel is far from easy. Streaming is a tough job that takes a lot of time, effort, and talent to be successful at. Even the biggest streamers have to put in long hours almost every day to stay at the top of the heap. They rarely take vacations, and if they start to lose popularity there will always be a new up-and-coming streamer to take their place. There is a lot of pressure, and it can be hard to handle.

Creating a basic Twitch channel is simple: all someone needs to do is sign up for an account and download the Twitch app. The only other required gear is a camera and a microphone. These things can come in many different forms. To stream directly from a phone, no special equipment is needed—everything is built into the device. Streaming from a gaming console such as a PlayStation or Xbox is also very easy. Controllers on modern gaming systems generally have built-in microphones. A camera is only needed if the streamer wants to appear onscreen.

With a modern console like a PlayStation 5, you can start a basic stream without any extra equipment.

Things can get more complicated when it comes to streaming from a PC. PC streaming generally requires a very powerful computer. This is because the computer has to run the game being played and record video and audio at the same time. Some streamers even use two computers at a time when streaming—one to play games on and another to handle the streaming part.

Those who stream from PCs usually also have webcams and microphones. Some top streamers often have

A high-quality microphone can make a streaming channel seem more professional to viewers.

Colored lighting can make a stream more exciting to watch.

very elaborate setups. More powerful cameras will
provide a clearer image, and a good microphone can
make the streamer sound better. High-quality lighting
can make the streamer look better on camera. Many
streamers also decorate the space around them,
creating an environment that viewers will enjoy looking
at. They might use colored lights to create a mood in
the room. Many of them place gaming posters, figurines,
and other collectibles in view of their cameras.

The Appropriate Age

Depending on how old you are, you may need to wait a few years before starting a streaming career of your own. Twitch and other services do not allow users under thirteen years old. And even after you turn thirteen, most states require all streamers to be supervised by a parent or guardian until they are eighteen. This means that only legal adults are allowed to stream unsupervised. It might seem unfair, but the rule exists to protect kids from adults who might try to hurt them.

Even with all the right gear, building an audience for a new streaming channel is very tough. There are a few tricks that can help, though. One is to set a schedule and stick to it. This allows viewers to know exactly when they should be tuning in. Another important thing is to stream often and consistently. This means streamers can't go for days without logging on. Most who are trying to hit the big time will stream almost every single day, especially early in their careers.

It's important for streamers to engage with their viewers. Most people don't just watch streams the way they watch TV. They want to get involved, chat with other viewers, and interact with the streamer. Good streamers thank viewers for subscriptions and donations, answer questions from the chat, and do their best to make everyone feel included.

Interacting with viewers is an important part of building a successful streaming channel.

Streamers also have to spend a lot of time promoting themselves on social media. This can be time-consuming and tiring. They might also try to connect with other, more popular streamers. This can be the quickest way to build up a new audience. If a more popular streamer invites a lesser-known streamer to play with them, it lets the newer streamer show off in front of a larger crowd than usual.

The most important part of playing games is always to have a great time!

Once a streamer has built an audience, they can finally start getting paid for their work. This means streaming for a certain number of hours per month, streaming on a certain number of different days per month, having a certain number of followers, and having a certain number of average viewers for each stream. Upon hitting these goals, Twitch will first allow a streamer to become a Twitch Affiliate. Hitting even higher numbers will allow streamers to become Twitch Partners. Only Affiliates and Partners are able to offer subscriptions for their channels and collect money from the ads that run on streams. This means that in the early days of starting a new channel, there aren't many ways to make money.

Of course, for a small number of talented streamers, the payoff is more than worth the hard work that goes into starting a channel. Have you ever thought about trying it one day? It won't be easy, but maybe you'll be one of the lucky few to hit the big time. You'll never know unless you try. And even if you don't, you'll still get to have fun playing games and chatting with friends online. There's no way to lose!

GLOSSARY

development (dih-VEL-uhp-muhnt) the process of making video games or other computer programs

engineers (en-juh-NEERS) people who design and build things

esports (EE-sports) organized, professional video game competitions

livestream (LAIV-streem) a live video or audio broadcast that takes place over the internet

moderators (MAH-duh-ray-turs) people who observe chat rooms to ensure that participants follow rules of conduct

pandemic (pan-DEM-ik) a widespread outbreak of disease

FIND OUT MORE

Books

Gregory, Josh. *Careers in Esports*. Ann Arbor, MI: Cherry Lake Publishing, 2021.

Loh-Hagan, Virginia. *Video Games. In the Know: Influencers and Trends*. Ann Arbor, MI: 45th Parallel Press, 2021.

Orr, Tamra. *Video Sharing. Global Citizens: Social Media*. Ann Arbor, MI: Cherry Lake Press, 2019.

Reeves, Diane Lindsey. *Do You Like Getting Creative? Career Clues for Kids*. Ann Arbor, MI: Cherry Lake Press, 2023.

Websites

With an adult, learn more online with these suggested searches.

Twitch.tv
Check out the biggest game streaming website in the world, where you will find people playing just about any game you can think of.

Facebook Gaming
Facebook's game streaming service isn't quite as big as Twitch, but it still has a lot of activity to check out.

INDEX